DATE DUE

JUNCT. 81 10 '90 *June*		

PATRICIA MALONEY MARKUN

THE PANAMA CANAL

A FIRST BOOK | REVISED EDITION
FRANKLIN WATTS | NEW YORK | LONDON | TORONTO | 1979

Photographs courtesy of Panama Canal Company

Library of Congress Cataloging in Publication Data

Markun, Patricia Maloney.
The Panama Canal.

(A First book)
Edition of 1958 published under title:
The first book of the Panama Canal.
Bibliography: p.
Includes index.
1. SUMMARY: Traces the development of the Pan-
ama Canal from the early planning stage through the
completion of construction.
1. Panama Canal—Juvenile literature.
[1. Panama Canal]   I. Title.
F1569.C2M36   1979   972.87   79–14510
ISBN 0–531–04075–5

CONTENTS

ONCE MORE, TO DAVE
WHO, AS LIEUTENANT DAVID J. MARKUN,
FIRST MATE OF THE FREIGHT SHIP
FS 313, USATC,
BROUGHT US IN ROUNDABOUT FASHION
TO THE PANAMA CANAL.

The author acknowledges appreciation for information and assistance to Governor Harold R. Parfitt, last governor of the Panama Canal Zone; to Frank A. Baldwin, Public Information Director of the Panama Canal Company; to Dwight A. McKabney, General Counsel; and to Captain Robert W. Haff, Jr., Deputy Chief, Transit Operations. Appreciation goes once more to Captain Jens Nilsen, retired Panama Canal pilot, whose knowledge and love of the ships of the world brought alive for me the adventure of the Panama Canal.

Air view of the Panama Canal

THE PILOTS "PUT A SHIP THROUGH"

It is five o'clock in the morning in the Panama Canal Zone—and very quiet. Suddenly Captain Tom Wright's telephone rings. At once he is awake.

"A driver will call for you in thirty minutes," a voice says, as the captain listens. "You will be taking the Norwegian freighter *Hoegh Mascot* through the canal northbound as number six transit."

It is the dispatcher from the marine control station in La Boca, Panama Canal Zone, giving the captain his orders for the day. Soon Captain Wright will be guiding a ship through the famous 50-mile (80.45-km) long waterway that connects the Atlantic and Pacific oceans. He is a Panama Canal pilot.

Forty-five minutes later he climbs into a white Panama Canal launch at a little dock outside Balboa, on the Pacific Ocean. He is wearing a white sport shirt and a baseball cap with a visor, for he will spend much of his day in the sun. He carries two small radios on shoulder straps.

Soon the little launch is tossing through rough waters in pre-dawn darkness on its way out to the deep waters. Twinkling lights mark the big ships at anchor. The launch weaves in and out among them—the Belgian *Ruth*, the *Hagaromo Maru* from Japan, the huge British freighter *Act Seven*, the Liberian tanker *Esso Saint John*, and many others —all waiting to go through the Panama Canal.

At last the launch comes alongside a very large gray, white, and blue freighter, marked *Hoegh Mascot* in white letters. Norway's red, white, and blue flag flies from her stern. The lights on the mast show a blue-and-yellow-striped pennant waving. In ship's language it means, "We request a pilot."

A rope ladder is thrown over the side of the *Hoegh Mascot*. The launch moves down to it carefully. Captain Wright stands on the edge of the tossing launch, holding the rail for support. The tiny craft rides up and down on the huge waves beside the towering ship.

The launch rises high on a wave crest. Captain Wright reaches out and grabs the hanging ladder. He holds on tight with hands and feet, then quickly scrambles upward. Beneath him the launch putt-putts away.

On the deck of the *Hoegh Mascot* a ship's officer in white uniform is waiting. He leads Captain Wright along flight after flight of stairs, high up to the place of command—the bridge of the ship. A tall man in a white uniform stands there. Four stripes on his sleeve show that he is the captain of the *Hoegh Mascot*. He greets Captain Wright and introduces himself as Egil Vambeseth. Then Captain Wright takes

[2]

command, and Captain Vambeseth moves back on the bridge. While any ship is going through the Panama Canal, the pilot is the captain in charge.

A member of the crew has taken down the "request a pilot" flag. In its place he now raises the pennant meaning number six and, beneath it, the half-red, half-white flag that means, "We have a pilot aboard." The number six flag means that the *Hoegh Mascot* is to be sixth in line going through the canal today. The number pennant's position *above* the pilot's flag means that the ship is northbound through the canal to the Atlantic Ocean. When a ship carries the number pennant *below* the pilot's flag, it is going south to the Pacific. Because of the way the narrow land neck of Panama lies, the canal runs nearly north and south.

Now on the forward mast of the *Hoegh Mascot* the flags of the United States and the Republic of Panama are raised. These are the "courtesy flags." All the ships of the world fly them when they travel through this waterway that was built by the United States and will belong to Panama in the year 2000.

When the *Hoegh Mascot* arrived at the canal's entrance yesterday, she put up the yellow quarantine flag. The Panama Canal's boarding officer made the first trip to the ship. The *Hoegh Mascot* had passed through the canal a few times before, so the boarding officer had a record of her "admeasurement"—that is, her size and the amount of cargo she could carry. With this information the officer could tell how much the ship should pay in tolls for passage through the canal.

The officer checked the kind of cargo aboard. If it had been explosive—munitions, fuel, or certain chemicals—special safety rules would have been enforced. He also checked to see if there was any illness aboard. If there had been smallpox, cholera, or any of a list of other contagious diseases, the ship would have been quarantined. In that case, she would not have been able to go through the canal for a certain number of days.

But the *Hoegh Mascot* passed inspection. Quickly the boarding officer added up the tonnage and calculated her tolls bill. The agent for the ship's owners had already paid to the Panama Canal treasurer the money to cover the tolls. The ship was cleared, and the yellow quarantine flag was lowered. Then she was free to request a pilot.

The Panama Canal is open to ships twenty-four hours a day. Because the *Hoegh Mascot* is a very large freight ship, she can transit only in daylight. As the sun begins to rise out of the Pacific Ocean, Captain Wright checks his watch against the ship's clock. It is ringing four bells, or 6 A.M.

"Slow speed ahead!" the pilot orders.

"Slow speed ahead!" the officer on watch repeats. The *Hoegh Mascot* moves through the waters of the anchorage into the canal channel.

No ship goes through the Panama Canal unaided. "Putting a ship through" is the job of the Panama Canal pilots. Most of them are licensed shipmasters before they train for six months to become pilots. Then for another year, as probationary pilots, they gain experience in taking some ships through the canal. After that year, they can pilot ships up to 526 feet (160 m) long. Additional training steps take them, in seven and one-half years, to the rank of senior pilot.

Guiding ships through this waterway takes special skill.

At Panama the waters of the Atlantic and Pacific oceans wash two coasts only 45 miles (72.4 km) apart. Here is one of the narrowest points on Central America's long, skinny neck. From Mexico to Colombia a mountain chain marches down the winding ridge of land. At the Panama Canal Zone these mountains dip to low hills, but the middle section of the zone is still quite high. Somehow the ships in the canal must climb across the high place, and only especially skilled pilots can guide them.

For about 7 miles (11.3 km) inland from the buoys that mark the Pacific entrance, the Panama Canal is at sea level. Tides here sometimes change the ocean level as much as 20 feet (6.1 m), but the canal is built so that ships navigate safely at high or low tide.

Likewise, from the breakwater on the Atlantic side of the Panama Canal Zone, ships go inland at sea level for about 6 miles (9.3 km). The difference in tides in this ocean is only about 3 feet (1 m).

Between these two sea-level channels lie Gatun Lake, a man-made body of water on the canal, and Gaillard Cut. This whole middle part of the canal is 85 feet (25.9 m) above sea level.

If the canal is to work, ships must be raised from the two sea-level channels to the higher level of Gatun Lake and Gaillard Cut. Then, once the ships have passed through the greater part of the canal at this high level, they must be lowered again to sea level.

The raising and lowering is done by three double sets of water stairs called "locks." A lock is a high-walled chamber with gates at each end, built into a canal. It works like this:

As a ship that is to be raised approaches the lock, the entrance gates open. At this time the water in the lock is at the same level as the water outside, where the ship is floating.

The ship enters easily, but once inside the lock the gates close. Now water pours into the lock through openings in its walls or floor. As the water level rises, the ship rises also until it is on a level with the higher part of the canal. Then the water stops rising, and the exit gates of the lock are opened. The ship floats out of the lock chamber and goes on its way.

If a ship is to be lowered, the lock works in the opposite way. The vessel enters a lock full of water. But once it is inside, the water runs out of the chamber until the ship is brought down to the lower canal level.

In the Panama Canal two water steps are placed together at Miraflores Locks near the Pacific end of the canal. These locks raise ships 54 feet (16.5 m) above sea level. Then the ships pass through small Miraflores Lake. They go up the final step at Pedro Miguel Locks. Now they are 85 feet (25.9 m) above sea level. To go down again on the Atlantic end, they pass through three chambers, or stairs, all built together at Gatun Locks.

No pumps are used to fill or empty the canal's lock chambers. The water simply runs downhill from Gatun Lake, which is ringed in by the solid banks of Gatun Dam. The lake level is higher than that of any of the locks before they are filled, so that the water runs into the locks easily. It flows from one level to another through large tunnels located in the middle and side walls of the locks. From these tunnels the water flows through smaller culverts opening into the walls and floors of the lock chambers.

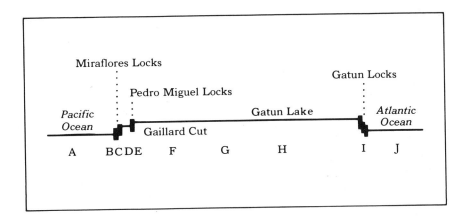

PROFILE OF THE PANAMA CANAL

A.   A ship approaches at sea level.

B.   At Miraflores Locks the first chamber raises the vessel 27 feet (8.2 m).

C.   The second chamber raises it up the water stairs another 27 feet (8.2 m).

D.   Now, 54 feet (16.5 m) above sea level, the ship proceeds 1½ miles (2.4 km) through Miraflores Lake.

E.   Pedro Miguel Locks' single flight raises the ship 31 feet (9.5 m). Now the ship has come 85 feet (25.9 m) above sea level. She will remain at this height for most of her passage through the canal.

F.   The ship moves through Gaillard Cut.

G.   At the town of Gamboa, the Chagres River enters the canal.

H.   Now the canal widens into Gatun Lake.

I.   At Gatun Locks the ship goes "down the stairs" to sea level again. In three steps, about 28 feet (8.5 m) at a time, the ship moves from lock chamber to lock chamber.

J.   At sea level once more, the ship goes through the 6-mile (9.3-km) channel that takes her out to the Atlantic Ocean.

[7]

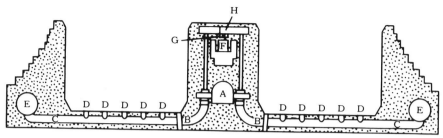

Cross section of lock chambers and walls, Gatun Locks

HOW A PANAMA CANAL LOCK IS BUILT

A.   Water pours through this huge culvert in the middle wall of the lock. The pipe is so large that a locomotive could go through it.

B.   Smaller culverts like this one run from A under the lock floor.

C.   Lateral culverts also come off large culvert E in the side wall of the lock.

D.   These wells, which run all along the lock floor, open into the culverts beneath them. When the wells are all open, water pours in or out of them quickly. In eight minutes 26 million gallons (98.8 million l) of water can pour in or out of the lock chamber.

E.   The large culvert running through the side lock wall.

F.   The drainage gallery in the middle lock wall.

G.   Electrical wiring runs through the lock wall. It carries current to operate gate and valve machinery.

H.   A passageway is built inside the middle lock wall for the lock operators.

To fill a lock the valves at the upper end are opened and the valves at the lower end are closed. The water flows from the upper pool through the large culverts into the small lateral culverts, and from there through the holes in the floor into the lock chamber. To empty a lock the valves at the upper end are closed and those at the lower end are opened. The water flows into the lower lock or pool.

[8]

To lift a ship up one single water step, 26 million gallons (98.8 million l) of water are needed. That is as much water as the whole of a medium-sized city uses in a day! Twice as much water—52 million gallons (197.6 million l)—is needed to take a ship all the way through the canal. But there is rarely a water shortage in the Panama Canal Zone. The Isthmus of Panama has a tremendous rainfall. The huge amount of water needed to operate the canal is stored in Gatun and Madden lakes during the long rainy season, and is used all the year through.

Now on the *Hoegh Mascot* Captain Wright orders, "Half ahead!" The officer pulls a lever called a "telegraph." It is marked with several speeds. He sets it at half speed, which is marked on this control in English and in Norwegian. By moving the telegraph on the bridge the officer signals the engine room far below. There the order will be carried out.

At the ship's bell book next to the telegraph another officer writes, "6:20 A.M. Hard starboard." Each order that the pilot gives during the trip through the canal will be recorded in the book.

The huge, new freighter moves easily into the channel, and passes dozens of little sailing boats and motor launches anchored at the Balboa Yacht Club. It sails under the high graceful arch of the mile-long (1.6-km) Thatcher Ferry Bridge which connects the two parts of Panama that the canal divides. In so doing, the bridge joins North and South America.

Now the pilot orders the ship to slow down for a launch that is coming alongside. Up the ladder come three more pilots—Captains O'Daniel, Olivares, and Hudgins. The *Hoegh Mascot* is a huge freight ship built particularly to carry container cargo. These containers are huge metal boxes 8 by 8 feet (2.4 by 2.4 m) by 40 feet (12.2 m) long. They are piled so high on deck that Captain Wright at the bridge cannot even see the front end of the ship. He will need the eyes of these three assisting pilots to move the ship safely through the narrow places in the Panama Canal.

Captain Wright, as senior pilot, stands on the middle of the bridge. Every couple of minutes he walks to the starboard (right) side of the bridge and looks down, carefully judging the position of the moving ship in the channel.

Captain O'Daniel comes up to the bridge and takes his post at the port (left) side. Captain Olivares walks around the deck cargo to the port side of the ship up at the bow (in front). On the starboard side of the bow, Captain Hudgins takes up his post.

As Captain Wright stands on the middle of the bridge, he can see the white tower and black gates of Miraflores Locks now approaching. Looking over the high-piled cargo, it seems impossible that this wide and heavy-laden ship will fit through those narrow lock gates.

But the super-size *Hoegh Mascot* and six sister ships were built just to fit through the Panama Canal locks. The ship is 101.3 feet (30.8 m) wide and about 658 feet (200 m) long. Passing through the locks, she will have about 4 feet (1.2 m) of clearance on each side of the ship. A lock is 110 feet (33.5 m) wide. Since each lock chamber is 1,000 feet (305 m) long, there is plenty of space for the length of the ship.

Now Captain Wright tunes in the two radios he brought

aboard. With one he will communicate with the pilots at the bow. With the other he can talk to the tugboats, to the locomotive operators (the Panama Canal mules), and to Transit Central.

He finds that one of his radios is out of order. He cannot contact the two pilots in the bow! Without that contact he certainly cannot start through the locks. Captain O'Daniel on the port side of the bridge contacts Transit Central. "Captain Wright needs a new crossbridge radio. Please send it out with the line handlers."

The ship slows down again and another launch comes alongside. Up the ladder file the men of the line-handling crew. They will secure towing cables to the ship when she reaches the locks. One of the men carries a new radio for Captain Wright.

The senior pilot turns on the new radio and tries to contact the pilots in the bow.

"I can hear you very well, Captain," comes the voice of Captain Hudgins on the radio. "Just try not to talk too much!"

The port has narrowed down to a 500-foot (152.5-m) channel. The ship has already gone more than 6 miles (9.7 km) in the canal.

"Stop!" orders Captain Wright.

"Stop!" echoes the officer, as he rings up the order on the telegraph.

The *Hoegh Mascot* slows down as her engines stop. Now the long concrete walls of Miraflores Locks surround her. A little rowboat comes alongside. It carries rope lines from the mechanical "mules"——the famous Panama Canal towing locomotives. A hundred years ago real mules towed ships through smaller canals, and the locomotives are often called "mules" even today.

The line handlers on the deck of the *Hoegh Mascot* throw down to the rowboat one end of a slender manila line called a "messenger." The man in the rowboat ties the messenger to the line from one of the towing locomotives. This is tied in turn to the steel towing cable from the mule. The deck crew now pulls up on the messenger line and on the heavier heaving line until the end of the steel cable from the locomotive is pulled up onto the ship. There the eye of the cable is thrown over a "bitt"—a steel fastening point on the deck of the ship—and the cable is made fast.

Being a large freighter, the *Hoegh Mascot* is a "six-locomotive lockage." This means that the ship needs six locomotives—three on each side—to take her through the locks. The two front mules do the actual pulling. The middle two help control the ship by pulling or braking as the pilot commands. The last two act only as brakes. With a ship this size, tugboats also help at both ends.

At last the steel cable from each mule is made fast. Now the lock gates, each one weighing 700 tons (630 metric tonnes), swing silently open. These gates are made of steel 7 feet (2.1 m) thick. They are not solid, though. Instead, they have hollow, watertight compartments. They almost float as they move open and fit snugly into the walls of the lock. Be-

LINE HANDLERS SCRAMBLE ABOARD
AS THE SHIP APPROACHES THE LOCKS.

THE PANAMA CANAL IS THE ONLY
WATERWAY IN THE WORLD THAT USES TOWING
LOCOMOTIVES. EIGHT "MULES" ARE NEEDED
TO TAKE THIS LARGE SHIP THROUGH THE LOCKS.

yond them the lock chamber appears. It comes almost as a surprise that the water level of the chamber ahead is exactly the same as the part of the canal where the *Hoegh Mascot* floats.

Two Panama Canal tugboats also help guide the big *Hoegh Mascot* into the lock. Responding to Captain Wright's orders, the agile tug *Rousseau* at the bow helps nose the ship into position, while at the stern the tugboat *Julian Schley* nudges the *Hoegh Mascot* to keep her steady in the lock. A tug in the rear is particularly helpful in steering a vessel when the pilot must reverse engines.

While the ship is moving through the locks, Captain Wright turns the direction of the mules over to Captain Hudgins. Standing up at the starboard bow, he can see much better than the senior pilot how the ship is moving ahead.

Captain Hudgins stands under a little canopy right at the edge of the ship. He gives orders to the mule operators, using his radio.

The mule operators answer, "I hear you," by ringing the locomotive bell.

Looking down over the side of the ship, Captain Hudgins sees that the starboard side of the ship is moving dangerously close to the middle wall. He radios to mule operators on the side wall, "One side support! Two side support!"

One bell and then another rings. The locomotive operators have pulled the lines as directed by Captain Hudgins. The ship moves no closer to the wall.

Very carefully the huge ship edges through the narrow lock chamber. The ship's engines help, too, and take some of the strain from the mules. All four pilots—each at a different part of the ship—look down every few seconds to see how evenly the *Hoegh Mascot* is moving between the narrow concrete walls. Water movements and wind can join to jar the ship out of its careful place in the middle of the chamber.

The big lock gates close behind the *Hoegh Mascot*. Now she is shut up in the 1,000-foot (305-m) long lock chamber, ready to "start upstairs" on the Panama Canal's "staircase over the mountains."

Up in the locks control tower the operator has been watching the *Hoegh Mascot*. He moved the switch that opened and closed the lock gates. Now he throws the switch that opens huge valves in the lock floor and middle wall. As if a stopper had been pulled from a bathtub, the water rushes out of the chamber ahead of the *Hoegh Mascot*. Water pours through culverts into the chamber where the ship now floats. Twenty-six million gallons (98.8 million l) of water enter the chamber in eight minutes. It comes in so smoothly that hardly a bubble shows on the surface. As the chamber fills with water, the ship rises. In eight minutes she comes up 27 feet (8.2 m). Now she is ready to go up a second step.

The lock gates open in front of her. There lies the second chamber, at exactly the water level the *Hoegh Mascot* has risen to. The pilot radios to the towing locomotives, and the mules answer with a "Ding" on their bells. The mules help guide the ship into the second chamber. When the lock gates are safely closed, the control operator moves a switch. Another 26 million gallons (98.8 million l) of water raise the *Hoegh Mascot* 27 feet (8.2 m) in eight more minutes. She is sitting 54 feet (16.5 m) above the level of the Pacific Ocean.

Now the *Hoegh Mascot* is ready to move out of the locks. The gates open. The locomotives move the ship through.

"Cast off! Thank you very much." Captain Wright radios the locomotive operators. The towing cables fall away from the ship. The pilot presses a button that blows the ship's whistle.

"Clear of the locks!" the whistle means. As if happy to escape that closed-in space, the ship advances out into the channel, into the open waters of Miraflores Lake.

When the *Hoegh Mascot* has gone about 1 mile (1.6 km), the pilot orders, "Stop the engines!" The ship has come to Pedro Miguel Locks. There is only one step here. Just as at Miraflores Locks, the ship rises—this time 31 feet (9.5 m). Now the *Hoegh Mascot* sits 85 feet (25.9 m) above sea level. She will travel at this height for almost all the rest of the way across the Isthmus. Just before reaching the Atlantic Ocean, she will go downstairs—one, two, three, to sea level—in Gatun Locks' three chambers.

Once the ship is clear of Pedro Miguel Locks, the pilot calls out, "Dead slow!"

The *Hoegh Mascot* is entering Gaillard Cut, the most treacherous stretch of the canal. Terraced green banks rise on either side of the channel. Between 1957 and 1962, the Cut was widened from 300 to 500 feet (91.5 to 152.5 m). Even so, it continues to be a tricky section of the canal to navigate.

Small ships do pass in the Cut, but very carefully. To do this, the ships go head-on toward each other. When they are a few hundred feet apart, each pilot heads the bow of his ship to starboard. As the ships pass, water currents may draw them dangerously close to each other. At the same time, currents pulling from the bank may draw the stern of the ship out of the channel toward the shore. The pilots must take care to keep their ships in the clear.

Very large ships—battleships, big passenger liners, tankers, and super-size container ships like the *Hoegh Mascot*—do not pass any other ship in the Cut. All traffic from the opposite direction stops while one of the giant ships goes through with a "clear Cut."

Hills rise higher on either side of the narrow channel as the ship reaches the high backbone of the land. Jungle grass now covers the scarred rock banks that rise on either side of the *Hoegh Mascot.* Each cubic yard of rock blasted out here took the mighty effort of dozens of canal construction workers.

On the left the *Hoegh Mascot* sails past the flat terraces of Contractors Hill. Trucks and power shovels flattened and terraced that hill in the 1950s. A deep crack had been found that threatened to send the whole hill sliding into the water.

Now the highest point along the canal looms above the *Hoegh Mascot.* It is the black rock of Gold Hill on the right. A landslide from this hill in 1974 sent about 1 million cubic yards (764,000 cubic m) of dirt into the Cut. Canal traffic was closed for several hours until it was determined that enough clearance remained for one ship at a time to proceed through that part of the Cut. Dredging began at once.

All through the Cut markers called "ranges" are posted to guide the pilots. The markers are black crosses painted on white signboards and placed in pairs, one above the other, in the hills. The pilot steers his ship so that the lower cross of

A TUG HELPS GUIDE THE SUPER-SIZE CONTAINER SHIP,
HOEGH MALLARD, THROUGH THE TREACHEROUS CUT.
AT THE RIGHT, A DRILLBOAT IS DEEPENING THE CANAL.

each pair appears to be lined up exactly with the one above it. By lining up the markers in this way he is sure to stay in the deep channel of the twisting Cut.

Captain Wright raises his binoculars and checks the distant pair of ranges. "Starboard ten . . . Midships . . . Ease to five," he commands. Minute by minute these brief orders shift the ship a few degrees to port or starboard to keep her in the middle of the canal channel.

The pilot's quiet orders and the officer's echo are the only sounds on the bridge. The officer patiently writes each order in the bridge's bell book. A radio squawk from Transit Central breaks in to report that a ship over on the Atlantic side has had steering gear failure. Captain Vambeseth, the Norwegian ship's captain, stands silent behind the senior pilot. He watches closely as this stranger who has taken command of his sleek, new ship guides her through the treacherous course. The Panama Canal is the only waterway in the world in which the pilot has full responsibility for all vessels.

At last the end of the dangerous Cut is in sight. The pilots relax a bit as the canal widens. The ship has passed safely through the Cut. On the right the Chagres River, source of much of the canal's water, flows into the canal. Beyond it lie the hillside houses of the town of Gamboa. On the left bank is the old steam dredge, *Las Cascadas*, huffing and puffing busily as it deepens the canal channel. Newer, more modern dredges have been brought to the canal and have worn out. But the old *Las Cascadas*, with its out-of-date steam engine, has been digging dirt out of the canal since it first opened.

The pilot orders the ship to increase speed to eight knots. Now the canal widens gradually, for here, where the Chagres

River enters, Gatun Lake begins. The *Hoegh Mascot* is sailing into one of the world's largest artificial lakes. It covers an area of almost 164 square miles (426.4 sq km), and was made by damming the Chagres River near the Atlantic Ocean. Now, instead of flowing into the sea, the water in the river has backed up and formed a huge lake. This lake supplies the water needed to operate the locks.

As Gatun Lake widens, it sprawls for miles in all directions. Buoys mark the course of the channel across the big lake—a strange, twisting course that follows the valley of the Chagres River, now lying far under water.

In Gatun Lake the channel is 1,000 feet (305 m) wide, so the *Hoegh Mascot* can go as fast as fifteen knots. It is past noon now. Captain Wright has been standing on the bridge for more than six hours. A steward appears with lunch trays for him and Captain O'Daniel. The pilots do not leave their posts, but eat right on the bridge. The pilots stationed in the bow go below deck to the ship's dining room for a brief lunch. They can relax while the ship is passing through Gatun Lake.

Captain Wright points out the site of the old town of Gorgona to the ship's captain as the *Hoegh Mascot* passes over it. Gorgona lay in the path of Gatun Lake. When the water began rising behind the dam, the town's residents were moved away. The remains of the village now lie buried under 80 feet (24.4 m) of water. Old mango trees stand on the shore of the lake. Behind them are banana groves gone wild. These trees were probably on the fringes of the town seventy years ago.

"Port five . . . Port ten . . . Midships."

The pilot's orders move the ship through the winding

THIS 1912 VIEW OF GATUN LAKE, ONE
OF THE WORLD'S LARGEST ARTIFICIAL
LAKES, SHOWS PART OF THE DYING JUNGLE.

channel. Her course takes her in and out among clumps of islands high with jungle grass. Skeletons of trees dead for sixty years stick up through the calm water just beyond the channel markers. Clusters of tropical orchids blister the gray trunks. These ghosts of the past remind passengers on ships that thick green jungle once grew where Gatun Lake's waters now ripple.

In a few minutes the *Hoegh Mascot* meets the first ship of the day, the *Irish Elm,* coming from the Atlantic. She is an Irish freighter, from Cork, bound for Japan, carrying a cargo of soybeans she took on in Florida. The *Overseas Alaska* in ballast, riding high and empty, goes by. She is a large tanker that carries oil from the Trans-Alaska Pipeline to the Gulf of Mexico by way of the canal. On this, her return trip, she carries no cargo.

The *Fairsea,* a handsome white passenger ship flying the British flag, glides by. Many tourists are out on the deck watching their ship proceed through Gatun Lake. Some of them wave to the people high up on the bridge of the *Hoegh Mascot.*

Gatun Lake gradually narrows, and the far end comes into view. Its jungle-clad shores hide the huge earthworks that hold back the lake's broad waters. On the left shore appears the broad concrete wall of Gatun Dam. Earth and concrete form the dike that keeps Gatun Lake from running down into the Atlantic Ocean.

To the right of the wall stands the white tower that marks Gatun Locks. The *Hoegh Mascot* has come to a traffic bottleneck in the canal. It is almost two o'clock in the afternoon. A few ships are still coming up the water stairs of Gatun

Locks—beginning the journey from the Atlantic to the Pacific. The pilot gives orders to drop anchor. There will be a wait before the *Hoegh Mascot* can go down to sea level.

The pilot walks out on the wing of the bridge. A line of ships stretches behind the *Hoegh Mascot* now, strung out in a row across Gatun Lake. They have followed her all the way through the canal. No ship overtakes another one in the Panama Canal. The ships behind the *Hoegh Mascot* must wait for her to be locked through.

At last the locks are clear. The pilot orders the anchor raised. Then he gives the command to go ahead. All four pilots are in their places as the ship moves into the triple lockage at Gatun. Once more the lock gates swing open, into one, two, three chambers with a drop or lift of about 28 feet (8.5 m) each. As if giant stoppers had been pulled, the water spills out of the Gatun Locks. The *Hoegh Mascot* rides down to sea level again in three giant steps.

As the last set of gates opens and the ship passes through, Captain Wright calls out, "Cast off lines! Thanks and good afternoon!"

"Ding, ding!" the locomotives answer him.

The towing locomotives' cables fall away. The *Hoegh Mascot* goes forward under her own power. At last she has reached the sea-level channel that will take her, shortly, to the Atlantic Ocean.

The remaining portion of channel goes by quickly. Then Captain Wright picks up his radio and reports to Transit Central.

"We are clear out of the locks and proceeding to the anchorage," he says. "No incidents. Good afternoon."

TWO SHIPS IN THE MILE-LONG, TRIPLE LOCKAGE
AT GATUN. THE DREDGED CHANNEL IN THE
BACKGROUND LEADS TO THE ATLANTIC OCEAN.

Soon a putt-putting alongside signals that the launch has arrived to take off the four pilots. Captain Vambeseth shakes hands with each of them with the silent understanding of shipmasters. Smiling, they say goodbye in English and Norwegian. The pilots' day of careful work is over. The *Hoegh Mascot* has reached the Atlantic Ocean safely and in good time. Captains Wright, O'Daniel, Hudgins, and Olivares go down the ladder and into the waiting launch. As it pulls away, Captain Vambeseth waves down to them from high up on the bridge. Once more he is in command of his own ship.

Down come the courtesy flag and the pennants—number six and "We have a pilot aboard."

"Full speed ahead!" the captain orders.

With a mighty blast of her whistle the *Hoegh Mascot*, guided safely from one ocean to another by skilled pilots, heads for the open sea. After ten days of clear sailing she will reach another continent. Across the high seas she is bound for Antwerp, port of Belgium, in Europe.

THE DREAM OF A WESTERN PASSAGE

It took ten years to build the Panama Canal before it was opened to shipping at last in 1914. For long years before that a path between the seas had been the dream of countless people. Christopher Columbus, on his fourth voyage to the Americas in 1502, sailed up and down Panama's coast looking for the magic passage to the West. He questioned the Indians at the mouth of the Chagres River, near where the canal now enters the Atlantic. Did they know of *another* sea near here? Yes, the Indians told his interpreters, there was such a sea. If Columbus would only leave his ships and follow them overland, they would show it to him. But Columbus said no. He ordered his crew to haul up anchor. He would reach that other sea by ship! He died without finding the waterway to the Orient.

Just a few years later, Vasco Nuñez de Balboa journeyed overland at Panama. This Spanish explorer found what Columbus would not leave his ships to discover. From a mountain peak in Panama's Darien Province, Balboa was the first white man to see the Pacific Ocean from the Americas.

Soon afterward the Spanish sailed all around the great pear-shaped continent of South America. And in their travels they learned the truth. There was no waterway between the continents. The mountains of Central America's ridge separated the oceans solidly, even at the narrowest places. Some explorers suggested that a canal be built across the isthmus. Spain's King Charles V was interested in the idea. By the middle 1500s four of the easiest routes had been marked out. Two were through Panama, one through Nicaragua, and one through what is now southern Mexico. However, four hundred years were to go by before the dream of a canal was to be carried out.

During the years when the Americas were being explored and colonized, there was only one way to reach the Pacific Ocean from the Atlantic by ship. That way was the long route around Cape Horn, the southernmost tip of South America. Captains and crews of whalers and China-bound clipper ships dreaded "rounding the Horn." From Panama's Atlantic coast a ship's crew could almost smell the Pacific Ocean, lying only 45 miles (72 km) west, over the horizon. But to reach the Pacific they had to sail down from the tropics and around the bulge of South America. Down, down they went for days and into the Temperate Zone again. As the weather grew colder, they reached the dangerous waters off Tierra del Fuego. There the currents of the Atlantic and the Pacific met, boiling up into sudden, terrible storms. Through cold and fog and between jutting reefs the ships sailed. Once around the tip of the Horn, they would begin the long journey up South America's west coast. But some vessels never reached the west coast. Instead, they smashed into Tierra del Fuego's reefs or capsized in its storms. Many a sturdy whaling ship and graceful clipper set off around the Horn from a northern port and was never heard from again.

Learning that another ship had been lost going around the Horn, people in the north would shake their heads sadly. If there were only a shortcut—a western passage between the Americas.

The discovery of gold in California in 1848 sent streams of people hurrying toward America's West. Many gold seekers journeyed across North America in covered wagons. Others, afraid of the fierce Plains Indians, took passage on ships going around the Horn. Some went the Panama route in the gold rush. By the hundreds they got off ships at the Chagres River in Panama. Little boats took them up that river to an old Spanish road, Las Cruces Trail. Going overland, they reached Panama City on the Pacific Ocean in two days. There they waited for other ships to take them north to California's gold fields.

In 1855, six years after the gold rush started, the first rail line across the Americas was completed—at Panama. Now a person bound for California could get on a crowded coach at the new town of Colon on the Atlantic. The wheezing, smoky train puffed across Panama on a single row of tracks. That afternoon, whistle blowing and bell ringing, it pulled into Panama City. Ocean to ocean in four hours. A western passage by rail was now possible!

Beginning with the gold rush, more and more settlers

A WAGON TRAIN TRANSITS BY FERRY IN 1933.

moved to the western part of the United States. Cities sprang up. Ranches and farms crisscrossed land that not long before had been Indian territory. Rail lines were built, and carried machinery and steel, cloth and plows to the West. And the trains brought back to the East beef and hides, wheat and ores.

But freight moves more cheaply by ship than by rail. And some things, too big for railway cars, still had to be carried around the Horn by ship. Many people in the United States talked of the need for a canal through Central America. Cheap trade between the east and west coasts of the United States would be a great help to the growth of the country and its commerce.

Other countries were interested in a canal, too. Every nation that owned a large merchant fleet talked of digging a canal between the Americas. What a saving of time and money it would mean to world trade.

Then, in 1869, the Suez Canal was cut between Africa and the Near East. Now ships would not have to go around Africa to get to Asia. Days of sailing time were saved as ships poured through the water ditch at Suez. Why couldn't the same thing be done in the Americas?

In 1878 a French company got a concession from Colombia to dig a canal across the Isthmus at Panama. The very man who had built the Suez Canal would head the job: Count Ferdinand de Lesseps. He sailed to Panama to begin his second canal.

De Lesseps and his workers soon found that the job at Panama was much harder than at Suez, where a wide ditch had been cut through flat desert sands. Panama had mountains. It had the wild, flooding waters of the Chagres River. Its Pacific Ocean had a 20-foot (6-m) tide while the Atlantic Ocean had a tide of only 3 feet (1 m).

Worse than all this, Panama's low swampland was one of the most unhealthful spots in the world. Yellow fever and malaria soon killed French workers by the hundreds.

De Lesseps' engineers worked on plan after plan for a canal that could go through the mountains, across a flooding river, and into two different tides. While they drew diagrams, their shovels and train engines rusted in the damp tropical weather.

Eight years after starting, the French gave up and fled the horrors of Panama. Their company had run out of money. They left behind some shallow ditches, deserted hospitals, and several cemeteries where thousands of workers lay buried. De Lesseps was brokenhearted. He died a few years later, forgetting his victory at Suez in his defeat at Panama. The French formed a new company and worked halfheartedly at the canal for some years. Then they abandoned this effort.

In 1898 the Spanish-American War began. Orders went out to the United States fleet to meet at once in the Atlantic. The battleship *Oregon* was cruising in the Pacific Ocean off California, guarding the western coast, when she received the message.

Starting from San Francisco, the *Oregon* went full speed ahead down around South America. Rounding the Horn, she steamed up the long east coast. It took the *Oregon* sixty-nine days to join the United States fleet in the Caribbean Sea. Now, as never before, people in the United States realized how much a canal through Central America was needed. With coasts on two oceans to defend, the fleet should have a short way to go from the Atlantic to the Pacific.

Many people thought that a canal should be dug at Nicaragua. An American company had tried unsuccessfully to dig a canal there in 1889. In 1897 the Walker Commission was appointed to study it and the Panama route. The Walker Commission recommended the Nicaraguan route, and in 1900 the House of Representatives voted to dig a canal across Nicaragua. The bill would next have to be approved by the Senate.

At this time, the French company that had failed in Panama and its American lawyer, William Cromwell, stepped in and convinced the Senate that the route across Panama would be cheaper, quicker, and less dangerous. The French company wanted $40 million for its rights and equipment in Panama.

Panama was at that time a province of the country of Colombia. Colombian officials pointed out to the Americans that the French concession was about to expire. They felt strongly that Colombia—not the French company—should be paid the $40 million. The Colombian Senate refused a United States offer of $10 million and an annual payment of $250,000 for the rights to dig a canal, made early in 1903.

Meanwhile, Phillipe Bunau-Varilla, who was chief engineer of the French company that failed, saw a way to get his company's money back. He knew that the people in the province of Panama had revolted several times to get their freedom from Colombia. He told the Panamanian patriots who wanted to revolt that the United States Navy ship *Nashville* would arrive in the port of Colon on November 3, 1903.

If the patriots revolted, the United States would enforce an old treaty it had with Colombia. Under that treaty, the United States had freedom of transit across the Isthmus of Panama. This would support the revolt.

The revolt took place as planned. The *Nashville* arrived on schedule. The Republic of Panama declared its independence from Colombia on November 3. Bunau-Varilla, waiting in Washington, had been named diplomatic agent by Panama to work out the agreement with the United States. Before two Panamanian diplomats arrived in the United States by ship, he had already negotiated the Hay-Bunau-Varilla treaty, with no Panamanians taking part. The Panamanian team took the treaty back to Panama City, and the new government approved it.

According to its terms, the United States guaranteed the little country's independence. In exchange, the Republic of Panama "grants to the United States all the rights, power, and authority within the zone (Canal Zone) . . . which the United States would possess and exercise as if it were the sovereign of the territory." The grant was "in perpetuity," which means forever.

From the very beginning, some Panamanians complained about the French-negotiated treaty. In 1904 the so-called Taft Agreements made some corrections. Major treaty revisions took place in 1936 and 1955, in which the United States paid Panama more money and gave other concessions.

At last, in 1978, the United States Senate ratified treaties to abolish the Canal Zone, pay Panama large amounts of money during the next twenty years, and to give the canal itself to Panama in the year 2000.

BUILDING THE CANAL

This strip of land named the Panama Canal Zone was to be used for building a canal, keeping it in working order, and protecting it. But could the job be done? Many intelligent people said no. With mountains, tides, rivers, fevers—building a canal was impossible, they declared.

One of the first Americans to arrive in the newly created Canal Zone was a friendly, energetic doctor, Colonel William Crawford Gorgas of the United States Army Medical Corps. Colonel Gorgas had just come from Cuba. There he had helped clean up the city of Havana after the Spanish-American War. He had been stationed in Cuba two years earlier when Colonel Walter Reed had discovered that a mosquito causes yellow fever.

Gorgas' job was to make Panama a healthful place to live. Carefully he explored the new area. Then he wrote to the United States government for the supplies he needed. He wanted to keep out mosquitoes by screening every door and window in the Canal Zone. The germs of cholera and other fevers were breeding in the filthy open sewers of Panama City and Colon; he asked for pipes to build modern sewers. He had to have equipment to pipe a pure water supply for Panama City, Colon, and the Canal Zone. He needed oil to spread on every stagnant pool of water where mosquitoes were breeding.

Colonel Gorgas waited for months, but his oil and screening and pipes did not come. Malaria and yellow fever began to kill the canal workers. The same hospital buildings where so many of the French had died were opened for the Americans. More and more men died, but only a small amount of screening arrived.

Meanwhile, in Washington, men were laughing at Gorgas' tremendous supply order. One official said, "Screening all the windows? He must want to turn the Isthmus of Panama into a summer resort!" He did not understand that protection by a screen could save a person's life when yellow fever and malaria mosquitoes were flying.

Then President Theodore Roosevelt heard about Colonel Gorgas' problem. He made sure that Gorgas got his screening. The oil and sewer and water pipes arrived in the zone, too. Workers' houses were screened. No one was allowed to go outside at night when the mosquitoes were biting. New sewers were built. Pure water was piped through the zone and into Colon and Panama City.

Very soon fewer people were becoming ill. One day in September, 1905, as an American worker lay dying of yellow

SPRAYING THE DITCHES WITH OIL
TO KEEP MOSQUITOES FROM BREEDING
IN THE EARLY CONSTRUCTION DAYS

fever in Ancon Hospital, Colonel Gorgas stood by with his fellow doctors. "Look carefully, men," he said. "This is the last case of yellow fever you will ever see."

He was right. There has never been another case of yellow fever in the Canal Zone. Cholera and smallpox disappeared, and there was much less malaria. The Canal Zone became one of the most healthful tropical spots in the world.

While Gorgas was making Panama a safe place to live in, engineers were planning the canal. Many questions had to be decided quickly. How wide should the canal be? Engineers knew that a sea-level canal from ocean to ocean would be best. But it would take too long to dig. How many locks should there be, then? How high must ships be raised to carry them over the hills? Could the Chagres River, with its floods and fury, be dammed up to make an artificial lake?

Many engineers came to the Canal Zone to help in the big job, but none of them stayed. At last, in 1907, President Theodore Roosevelt named Colonel George W. Goethals of the Army Engineers to head the task.

"An army man," the President said, "will go where he is sent, and he will *have* to stay. The canal *must* be dug!"

Colonel Goethals stayed. President Roosevelt made it clear that Goethals was the boss. He was in charge of the thousands of construction workers who were digging the canal. The Colonel was ready to work as hard as any of his men. He was willing to hear their complaints, too. Every Sunday morning at ten o'clock any worker with a problem could come to see him. Dozens of workers stayed on the job because of the Colonel's help in his Sunday-morning chats.

But even the Colonel was discouraged by the landslides.

Workers would dig away for weeks into the side of Gold Hill or Contractors Hill. After dynamite had been placed and had blown the face of the rock into pieces, clumsy steam shovels would trundle in to eat away at the broken boulders. Just when a good-sized ditch had been dug, a landslide would begin. A sudden rain might start it, or a loud noise, or perhaps nothing that anyone could see or hear. With a loud crash, part of the hill would slide into the new ditch like a terrible waterfall. The heavy fall of earth would bury men in their steam shovels.

Workers were killed; weeks of work spent in vain. With more dynamite and other steam shovels the crews would begin again.

At last, in 1914, the canal was finished. Bright new concrete walls marked three sets of locks—two on the Pacific end of the canal, and one on the Atlantic. A huge dam now plugged the mouth of the wild Chagres River. Behind it rose one of the world's largest artificial lakes.

The freight passenger ship *Ancon* was chosen for the first official transit of the canal. This vessel had brought hundreds of workers to their jobs in the Canal Zone. Early on the morning of August 15, 1914, the *Ancon* started from the Atlantic Ocean into the newly-cut channel. A few hundred lucky construction workers crowded aboard her for the historic trip. Other hundreds on the Atlantic shore waved to the *Ancon* as she steamed up the channel. Whistles and bands hailed her passage. At Gatun Locks the shiny new towing locomotives came to meet the ship. The lock gates opened for transit number one. Crowds cheered as the ship moved into the lock chamber. The gates swung closed.

ABOVE: THERE WAS GREAT COMPETITION BETWEEN
STEAM SHOVEL OPERATORS WHO ARE SHOWN HERE
MEETING AT THE DEEPEST PART OF THE CUT.
RIGHT, TOP: CULEBRA CUT UNDER CONSTRUCTION.
RIGHT, BOTTOM: CULEBRA CUT BEING DREDGED IN 1913.

The signal was given to fill the lock chamber. Water rushed in; the chamber filled; and the ship rose 28 feet (8.5 m). The gates opened and the ship moved into the second chamber. Up she went—and out! Again she repeated her rise. The "staircase over the mountains" was a success!

On through the canal the ship went. All along the route people watched her progress. Late that afternoon she entered the Pacific Ocean in triumph. Whistles blew. Flags waved. Crowds cheered. The *Ancon* had gone from the Atlantic to the Pacific in eight and one-half hours.

Building the Panama Canal had taken many years, many millions of dollars, and many lives. But Columbus' dream of a western passage had come true. At last the land had been cut and the oceans joined.

KEEPING THE CANAL RUNNING

When the great job of building the Panama Canal was finished, General Goethals received special recognition. The President of the United States appointed him the first governor of the Panama Canal Zone. From then on, each governor was appointed for a four-year term from General Goethals' outfit, the Corps of Army Engineers. The last governor, Major-General Harold R. Parfitt, was appointed by President Ford in 1975.

Under the treaties, as of October 1, 1979, the Canal Zone will no longer exist, and the Panama Canal Company and the Canal Zone government must stop operating in Panama. Their functions are to be taken over by a new United States government agency called the Panama Canal Commission, by other United States government agencies, or by the Republic of Panama.

The Board of Directors of the Panama Canal Commission is to be made up of five Americans and four Panamanians. Until 1990, the Administrator (the chief executive officer of the Commission) will be an American, and the Deputy Administrator, a Panamanian. After that, a Panamanian will serve as Administrator, and an American as Deputy. The Commission will handle only services that affect the canal directly.

Running this waterway for the world is expensive. In addition to the day-to-day work of getting the ships through, there is the cost of repairs and upkeep. Three sets of locks must be kept working smoothly. Every few years they must be overhauled, scraped free of barnacles, and parts must be cleaned and greased. A large force of pilots must be trained to take ships through. The channel must be dredged constantly to keep it at least 42 feet (12.8 m) deep.

Many specialists are needed to keep the canal working. Pilots, dredging engineers, lockmasters, tugboat operators, and shipfitters are only a few of them. Only twenty-eight percent of jobs were held by United States citizens at the time of the treaties-signing. Panamanian citizens have first chance at jobs under the new treaties.

The Canal Zone's hospitals and schools will be operated by the Department of Defense under the new treaties. Any new United States employees brought down by the Commission will be on a five-year rotation plan that will take them back to the United States. For the first five years of the treaty, United States citizen employees of the Commission will have access to military postal and commissary services.

When the treaty goes into effect, Panama will be sovereign in what was the Canal Zone, although United States

GATUN DAM IS RARELY SEEN SPILLING WATER LIKE
THIS, FOR WATER IS ONE OF THE MOST CRITICAL
ITEMS IN THE OPERATION OF THE PANAMA CANAL.

courts will keep limited jurisdiction after that date over certain United States citizens until April 1, 1982. Only Panama's police, courts, and prisons will operate in Panama.

In October of 1979, Panama will take over the customs and immigration, some fire protection, and operation of the ports of Balboa and Cristobal. Panama will also start running the coast-to-coast rail line. It will also operate the ship repair facility that has been owned by the Panama Canal Company.

In exchange for continuing to operate the Panama Canal until the year 2000, the United States is paying large sums of money to the government of Panama. Every year an outright fee of $10 million will be paid. Also, Panama will receive thirty cents for every ton of cargo space on ships that go through the canal. The Panama Canal Commission will pay a fixed fee of $10 million to Panama for services, such as police and fire protection, rubbish collection, and road maintenance in certain areas. If, after these payments, the Panama Canal Commission has additional money, Panama will get up to another $10 million.

Whatever Panama earns from the canal enterprise under the new treaties will be drawn entirely from canal revenues. There will be toll increases to cover this. Exactly how much, no one knows. Some guesses are that it will be about a thirty percent increase to begin with.

Under the terms of the new treaties, the Panama Canal will forever remain neutral. During a war, for instance, it would be open to all the ships of the world on terms of entire equality. Warships and other military vessels of the United States and Panama will always have a right to go to the head of the line through the canal. During the years until the end of the century American military forces will continue to control various forts, air bases, and military areas in the lands that were the Canal Zone. The United States has the right to assure militarily that the canal remains open, neutral, secure, and accessible.

Starting with the year 2000, operation of the canal will be the responsibility of the Panamanians. By then it is expected that Panamanians will have moved into all levels of management. At the time of the treaties-signing, only two Panamanians were qualified as Panama Canal pilots. In the years until Panama takes over, young Panamanians will be encouraged to spend several years in maritime academies and later at sea to become shipmasters. Then such a person would qualify for the long training needed to learn the complicated techniques involved in taking ships of all kinds and sizes through the canal.

WHO USES THE CANAL?

Big passenger ships carrying tourists on tropical cruises are exciting to watch as they pass through the canal. But they are rare birds that pass chiefly during the winter months of the tourist season. Before air travel became so fast and cheap, passenger ships were daily visitors to the Panama Canal. Shipping companies with several ships transported hundreds of passengers weekly between England and Australia or New Zealand through the canal. Other companies provided regular passenger service between North and South America.

Now people journey all over the world by air, carrying new ideas and new ways of living to underdeveloped lands. The materials to build up those nations move as ocean freight on ships. Road-building machinery, dredgers to make new ports, steel for new buildings, drilling rigs to find untapped oil—all travel by ship. Much of that cargo goes through the canal.

The freight ships of the world are the canal's chief users. They funnel through the waterway from seventy or more different trade routes. The money they save by using this shortcut amounts to millions of dollars a year.

Many ships that pass through the canal with cargos bound for the United States carry raw materials. Ores, fuel, and other materials are needed to feed the busy American factories. Certain things must be brought in from outside because the United States does not have them at all. Rubber comes through the canal shortcut from Indonesia; coffee from Colombia, Chile, and Peru; tin from Chile and Peru.

Grain was the number one cargo carried through the canal in 1977. More than 23 million tons (20 million metric tons) of grains moved through the Panama Canal, chiefly from the United States to countries all around the world. Over 10 million tons (9 million metric tons) of the grain was corn exported from eastern United States to Japan. In that year Japan also imported by way of the Panama Canal 4½ million tons (4 million metric tons) of American soybeans.

The most popular trade route by far is between East Coast United States and countries of Asia, particularly Japan. Japanese ships go through the canal almost every day. They take manufactured goods to the eastern coasts of the United States and South America. Then back to Japan they hurry with the coal, pig iron, and steel bars that their own country lacks.

The second most popular trade route through the canal is between the western coasts of the United States and Canada to Europe. This route involves much shipment of Canadian timber and pulpwood, fresh and frozen fruits and vegetables

THE JAPANESE CONTAINER SHIP
TOKYO BAY DWARFS THE AVERAGE-SIZE
FREIGHTER IN THE OTHER LOCK.

from the United States, chemicals from the United States, and manufactured goods from Europe.

The passageway between the oceans has helped to build up countries far from the canal. Chile, for instance, depends on the Panama Canal as if it were a lifeline. Soon after the waterway opened, nitrate mining became a thriving industry in that country. This mineral for fertilizer was loaded on ships and funneled through the canal to the eastern United States and to Europe.

Now nitrates have been replaced by artificial fertilizers, but today Chile trades other cargos as well. Out of the country's rich earth thousands of tons of valuable copper, tin, and nickel are mined each year. These minerals are shipped to the United States, England, Italy, and Germany by way of the Panama Canal.

Everything from safety pins to huge steel derricks appears on the cargo lists that ships must present before they enter the canal. By watching the cargos, a person can trace what is going on all over the world.

When the Arab-Israeli War closed the Suez Canal last in 1967, dozens of strange ships appeared for the first time at Panama. Australian, Nationalist Chinese, and Russian ships— all used to running regularly through Suez—arrived at the outer anchorages. Some of these ships were like an embarrassed student at a new school. They were newcomers who didn't know the rules. They all had to be admeasured, since the Panama Canal had no record of their measurements. They had to choose ship's agents to arrange for tolls payments. The crew members who had not been through the Panama Canal before were often surprised to see how complicated the canal was compared to the Suez. The Suez Canal, having no locks, is an easy, wide ditch through flat desert. Using the Panama Canal with six lockages, they found, was much more complicated.

The United States involvement in the Vietnamese War brought a great increase in Panama Canal traffic. At the time, the Suez Canal was still closed. The number of ships and amount of cargo passing through the canal broke all records in the early 1970s.

Many headlines in today's papers will be felt in the Panama Canal traffic a month from now. What ships are using the canal? What cargos are they carrying? Where are they taking their loads? The answers to these questions can change from day to day. When the fruit crop fails in Italy and Spain, ships file through the waterway with extra banana shipments for Europe. If a famine strikes in India, ships carrying wheat to starving people hurry through the shortcut.

A freight ship blasts its tremendous whistle as it steams into the Panama Canal. Somewhere, perhaps halfway around the world, something has happened in business or politics to to send that ship cruising through the winding waterway. Weather, a revolution, crop failure, a business boom or a depression—all can be marked and charted by the changing line of traffic through the Panama Canal.

The completion of the Trans-Alaska Pipeline in 1977 had a direct effect on the Panama Canal within a few weeks. Oil pumped from Alaska's snowy North Slope flowed across that huge state by the pipeline and was loaded into supertankers at the south Alaskan port of Valdez. The tankers then journeyed down the West Coast, past Mexico and Central

IT'S A TIGHT FIT IN THE PEDRO MIGUEL
LOCKS FOR THE GIANT CONTAINER SHIP *BENEVON*.

America and anchored off the coast of Panama. From there the oil was pumped into other tankers serving as oil-storage terminals. Finally it was transferred into tankers small enough to fit the 1,000 by 110 foot (305 by 33.5 m) measurements of the Panama Canal locks. These tankers took the oil through the canal to the refineries on the Gulf Coast.

A few months after the pipeline went into full operation, three tankers were going through the Panama Canal on the same day. In all they were carrying nearly 1,200,000 barrels of Alaskan oil through the waterway that day! Eventually a pipeline starting from California may carry much of this oil eastward. But the year the Trans-Alaska Pipeline went into operation, oil became the second-ranked cargo going through the canal.

The reopening of the Suez Canal in 1975 brought an almost instant drop in the amount of Panama Canal traffic. Ships going from Europe to Asia disappeared from the daily published list of canal users. It was shorter to go from Europe to Asia by way of the Panama Canal than to sail all around the continent of Africa. But reopening the Suez Canal made that route by far the shortest way.

The size of the average ship going through the Panama Canal is gradually increasing. Ship owners have found that one big ship can carry more cargo at less cost than a couple of smaller vessels. For the canal this means more "clear Cut" transits. These take more time and keep every ship waiting while a big one goes through Gaillard Cut alone. It also means the time of more pilots to take big ships through. If and when ships outgrow the size of the canal, a new and larger one will have to be dug somewhere between North and South America.

THE CANAL
OF THE
FUTURE

The concrete lock walls in the Panama Canal stand only 110 feet (33.5 m) apart. This restriction is beginning to raise a great problem for the future of the waterway.

When the locks were built, Goethals and his fellow engineers did not dream of the huge size of today's ships. And the canal's engineers faced a problem. Would lock gates wider than 110 feet (33.5 m) be strong enough to stand up to the strain of constant opening and closing? It was thought wisest not to chance too great a width.

For many years, as stronger engines made it possible to build larger vessels, ship designers all over the world carefully remembered the measurements of the Panama Canal locks. "One hundred and ten feet [33.5 m] by one thousand [305 m]," they said to themselves as they drew plans for new ships.

[55]

THE *TARAWA*, AN AMPHIBIOUS ASSAULT VESSEL,
IS THE LARGEST U.S. NAVAL VESSEL NOW IN
SERVICE THAT CAN TRANSIT THE PANAMA CANAL.

The huge passenger ship, the *Queen Mary,* launched in 1936, was 118.5 feet (36.1 m) wide. She was 8.5 feet (2.6 m) too broad in the beam—the first ship ever built too wide ever to pass through the Panama Canal locks. But that fact was not important. She and her sister ship, the *Queen Elizabeth,* which was launched a little later, were designed especially for transatlantic service. They would not need to use the canal.

During World War II the United States Navy launched giant aircraft carriers and enormous battleships. In building all of them, designers remembered the lock measurements of the Panama Canal. No ship must be too wide to pass through that waterway.

All the battleships of the United States fleet can go through the Panama Canal, although they need the help of five pilots to do it. One pilot stands on the bridge and four others are spaced around the ship. They give orders by portable radio as the battleship moves through the locks with only inches to spare. The screeching and scraping can be heard for a mile (about 1½ km) away as a towering gray monster like the 108-foot (32.9-m) wide *New Jersey* is tugged through by ten straining locomotives. Paint has been scraped off the hulls of battleships. The wooden fenders that protect the concrete walls have been splintered. But no big damage has ever been suffered by these giants of the fleet as they passed through the canal.

Aircraft carriers have an angled flight deck to give the fighter planes more landing room than if the landing strip just went the length of the carrier. The angled landing makes the flight deck wider than 110 feet (33.5 m)—too wide to pass through the canal.

At least two dozen VLCCs (Very Large Crude Oil Carriers) or supertankers are too wide, too long, and too deep to fit through the Panama Canal. If the canal were bigger, the oil from Alaska could pass through the canal in supertankers without having to be pumped into smaller tankers that can fit through the locks.

Container cargo has quickly become the popular way to move ocean freight, and larger freighters are being constructed to transport the containers. Panama Canal engineers can see that someday the canal may be too narrow for the trade that uses it most.

Many new ships that will fit the locks are too big to pass another ship in Gaillard Cut. Traffic through the canal is sharply slowed down when Gaillard Cut becomes a "one-way street." Sometimes, while one ship has a "clear Cut," fifteen or eighteen others must wait in Miraflores Lake or Gatun Lake.

When three or four "clear Cut" ships arrive in one day, the marine traffic control staff has a real problem. They look at their control computer as if it were a tight game of chess. What ship should move first in order to save the most time for every vessel? Every ship goes through the canal so that it may save time. Time is money on the high seas, for a crew must always be paid, and perishable cargo moved quickly.

Gaillard Cut has been widened and dredged to 500 feet (152.5 m). But the concrete locks cannot be stretched an inch. The problem of the future is: how can the Panama Canal be enlarged?

The United States Congress took some first steps toward enlarging the canal in 1939. The plan was to build a third set of locks alongside the present ones. Work was started, but stopped after the United States entered World War II. At that time it was important that everyone work to help the war effort.

Congress studied the problem of the canal again in 1947. The effects of bombing during the war had raised a new question. Since one good-sized bomb could destroy the locks, should a lock canal be built at all? Many people felt that the best way to improve the canal would be to dig a new one from ocean to ocean *at sea level*. Then there would be no locks, no dam, and no artificial lake to be protected from air attack.

The sea-level canal plan is for a broad, open waterway, free of dangerous curves, and 600 feet (183 m) wide. It would be about 5 miles (8 km) shorter than the present canal. Ships could pass through it in half the time they take today, and even big ships could pass each other in its channel.

But what about the big difference in the tides of the two oceans? With a 20-foot (6-m) Pacific tide and a 3-foot (1-m) Atlantic tide, would the canal between them stir up dangerous water currents? It has been decided that ships could navigate in spite of the currents. But a tidal lock would make their passage safer. The lock would operate only when the tidal currents ran high. Except for the tidal lock, there would be clear sailing from ocean to ocean.

A sea-level canal would cost a vast amount of money and would take ten years to dig. Traffic on the present canal would not be closed during that time except for seven days at the very end. In that last week, land plugs would be removed from the channel near each ocean, and Gatun Lake would run out into the sea.

The Panama Canal treaties commit the United States

PANAMA CANAL TUGS GIVE THEIR
TRADITIONAL SALUTE TO THE CRUISE SHIP
GOLDEN ODYSSEY AS IT PASSES UNDER THE THATCHER
FERRY BRIDGE AFTER ITS SOUTHBOUND TRANSIT.

and Panama to study the possibility of building another canal through Panama. If they agree it is necessary, they will negotiate terms for its construction.

Other engineers prefer another plan for the canal. This calls for a new set of larger three-chamber locks at Gatun and a three-step set at Miraflores. Pedro Miguel Locks would not be rebuilt. The lake behind Miraflores Locks would be raised to the same level as Gatun Lake. Under the new treaties, the United States has the right to build a third set of locks.

Deciding how to make the canal bigger and when to do it is the problem of the United States Congress. Pilots continue to put ships carefully through the waterway. Accidents are bound to happen now and then as bigger ships geared to higher speeds move through the narrow locks and dangerous channel. Although relatively few accidents are very serious, a ship runs aground or scrapes a lock wall about once every nine days.

Yet the Panama Canal of today stands as a modern miracle of engineering genius. Without any major changes it has worked well since 1914. The trade of the world moves through it; and the commerce of the United States depends on it. Peoples have been brought closer together by it; and it has helped make a better life for millions who live along the trade routes it serves. The oceans have been joined, and a passageway made through the Americas.

PANAMA CANAL FACTS AND FIGURES

DISTANCES

	MILES	KM
Airline distance between Balboa on Pacific and Cristobal on Atlantic	36	57.9
Length of canal, deep water to deep water	50	80.5
Shoreline distance of Gatun Lake	1,100	1,769.9
Distance saved by ships, New York to San Francisco	7,873	12,667.7

DIMENSIONS

	FEET	M
Length of each lock chamber	1,000	305.0
Width of each lock chamber	110	33.5
Depth of each lock chamber	70	21.4
Minimum depth of water in each lock	40	12.2
Width of each lock gate leaf	65	19.8

	FEET	M
Height of lock gates	47–82	14.3–25.0
Thickness of each lock gate leaf	7	2.1
Diameter of main culverts to fill locks	18	5.5

NUMBERS

Towing locomotives used for each ship	4 to 10
Daily average total passages (for 1978)	35.9
Total ocean-going commercial passages in 1978	12,991
Total canal passages of all vessels to December 31, 1978	556,758
Tons of cargo shipped through the canal in 1978	151,488,000 long tons

OTHER BOOKS
TO READ

Dolan, Edward F., Jr., and Silver, H. T. *William Crawford Gorgas: Warrior in White.* New York: Dodd, Mead, 1968.

Hadfield, Charles. *Canals of the World.* New Rochelle, N.Y.: Soccer Associates, 1964.

Markun, Patricia Maloney. *The First Book of Central America and Panama.* New York: Franklin Watts, 1972.

McCullough, David. *The Path Between the Seas: The Creation of the Panama Canal 1870–1914.* New York: Simon and Schuster, 1977.

Ransom, P. J. *Your Book of Canals.* London: Faber and Faber, 1977.

Sterling Editors. *Panama and the Canal Zone in Pictures.* New York: Sterling, 1969.

INDEX